Virginia Satir

SELF
ESTEEM

CELESTIAL ARTS
BERKELEY, CALIFORNIA

Copyright ©1970, 1975 by Virginia Satir

Published by Celestial Arts, P.O. Box 7123, Berkeley, CA 94707

Cover design by: Toni Tajima

First printing: September, 1975
Manufactured in the United States of America

Library of Congress Cataloging in Publication Data

Satir, Virginia M.
        Self-esteem.

        1. Self-respect.   l.Title.
BF697 .S25 158'.1 75-9447
ISBN 0-89087-109-4

26 27 28 29 30 — 00 99 98 97 96

SELF
ESTEEM

Art by Claudia Ricketts and David Mitchell

PROLOGUE

At this writing I have been a therapist and teacher for nearly 40 years. Once in a while in my life, things come together in a new way. This is a point of creation for me. I see myself in my world through different glasses. This continues until some further new pieces come together and again with the new glasses I see me in my world differently. Writing the poem which you are about to read was one such point for me.

It was a Tuesday afternoon in early spring in Palo Alto, California. The air was fresh and the sun was coming through the open window. The breeze gently blowing on the curtain made lively reflections and shadows were playing on the walls in the room that was my office. Maria, an attractive, eager, yet somewhat worried and sometimes very angry 15-year-old girl, was sharing this time with me. Maria and I had become good friends.

There was a strong bond of trust that had developed during the three years we had known each other. We had met when Maria was 12. She was desperate over how to find her way among all the puzzles, pains and struggles with which she was living in her family—a situation many of you who are reading this may know something about. At one point in the middle of Maria telling me about a very hurtful experience with her mother she looked at me helplessly and desperately and said through angry tears, "What is life all about anyway? Life makes no sense. What is the meaning of it all?" At that moment, in that situation and where I was in my life, there with Maria, her questions had a powerful impact on me. I felt deeply stirred and at the same time uneasy.

Her words were not strange to me, her questions were not unfamiliar. I had said the words myself and had heard them from others. I don't know whether I had ever put the question to myself just like that before. If I had I had not remembered my answer. I loved Maria and felt her pain very deeply. I wanted to help her. Maybe if she could find some kind of an answer for herself to a very central human question she might have a new place to begin. I knew that to give something to her I had to answer the question for myself. I then realized that I never really had. The poem "I Am Me" was my answer then.

Fifteen years have passed since I wrote that poem. For both Maria and me it was the beginning of whole new possibilities. Furthermore, during these past fifteen years many people have read the poem. There were so many people who said: "Reading your poem put so many things in place for me. Can I have a copy and give it to my friends?" The requests became so numerous that publishing it seemed to be the next step.

I

am

me

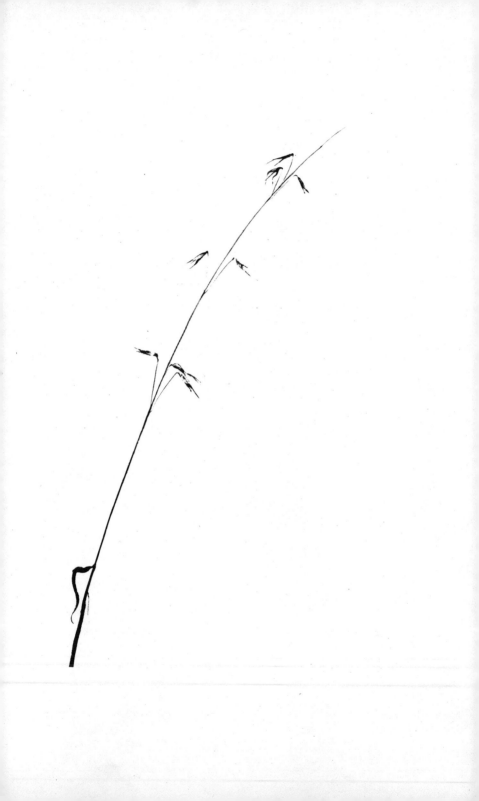

In all
   the world,
there is
no one else
   like me.

there are persons
who have some parts like me,
but no one
adds up exactly
like me.

Therefore,
everything that comes
out of me
is authentically mine
because
I alone chose it

I

   own

      everything

   about

   me

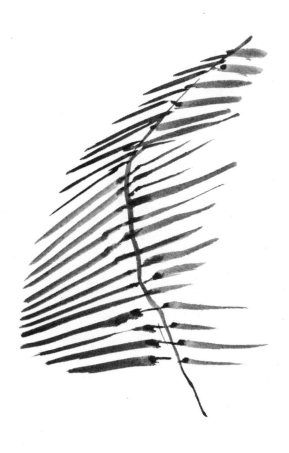

my body,

including
everything
it does;

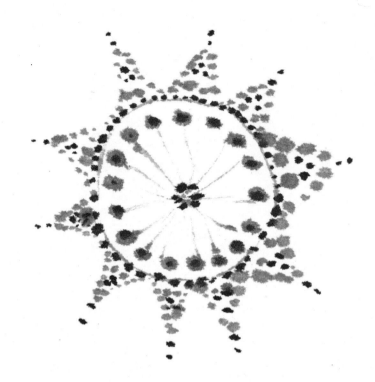

my mind,

including
all its
thoughts and ideas;

my eyes,

including
the images
of all they behold;

my feelings,

whatever they may be

anger,
joy,
frustration,
love,
disappointment,
excitement;

my mouth,
    and all the
words that
    come out of it,

    polite,
    sweet or rough,
    correct or incorrect;

my voice,

      loud

         or

      soft;

and all my actions,

whether they

be to others

or

to myself.

I own

> *my*
> *fantasies,*
> *my*
> *dreams,*
> *my*
> *hopes,*
> *my*
> *fears.*

I

   own

      all

         my

            triumphs

            and

            successes,

      all

         my

            failures

            and

            mistakes.

Because I own
all of me,
I can
become intimately
acquainted with me.

By so doing
I can love me
and be friendly with me in all my parts.
I can then
make it possible for all of me
to work in my best interests.

I know
there
are
aspects
about
myself
that
puzzle
me,

and
other
aspects
that
I
do
not
know.

But as long as
I am friendly
and loving to myself,

I can
courageously and hopefully
look for the
solutions to
the puzzles and
for ways to find
out more about
me.

However I look and sound,
whatever I say and do, and
whatever I think and feel
  at a given moment in time
    is
      me.

This is authentic and
represents where I am
  at that moment in time.

When
  I
review
    later
how
I looked and sounded,
what I said and did,
and how I thought and felt,
    some
      parts
        may
          turn
            out
              to
                be

unfitting.

I
can discard
that which
is unfitting,
and keep
that which proved
fitting,

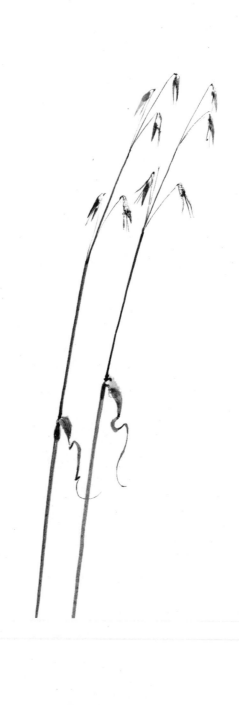

and
invent
something
new
for
that
which
I
discarded.

I can

> *see,*
> *hear,*
> *feel,*
> *think,*
> *say,*
> *and do.*

I have the tools

   to survive,
      to be close to others,
         to be productive,

   and to make sense and order
   out of the world of people
   and things outside of me.

*I
own
me,*

and

therefore

I

can

engineer

me

I
am
me

and

I

am

okay.

AFTERWORD

I AM ME

Maybe you now are in that situation,
that place in your life,
and with that awareness of yourself,
that the poem had impact on you too.

Maybe you experienced while reading it
what other people have.
Namely, that your value of yourself,
the new possibilities
of guiding and enjoying your life,
and getting closer to yourself
as the miracle that you are is enhanced.
You can see how your life can take on
new directions for yourself.

For me, anything that gives new hope,
new possibilities and new positive feelings
about ourselves
will make us more whole people
and thus more human, real and loving
in our relationships with others.
If enough of this happens,
the world will become a better place
for all of us.
I matter.
You matter.
What goes on between us matters.
Since I always carry me with me,
and I belong to me,
I always have something to bring
to you and me—
new resources,
new possibilities to cope differently
and to create anew.

Lovingly,

Virginia Satir

Books:

MAKING CONTACT shows how you can understand the basic tools for making contact with others and explains how you can use them to work for change in your perceptions, your actions, and your life.

MEDITATIONS & INSPIRATIONS is a collection of simple stage-setting monologues Virginia delivered to workshops all around the world. Her colleagues John Banmen and Jane Gerber have gathered the most popular of these inspirational pieces from over twenty-five years.

YOUR MANY FACES offers Virginia's central theme developed in more than forty years as therapist, author, lecturer, and consultant. She demonstrates that your "many faces" reveal the *real* you and recognizing them may open the door to change in your life.

Posters:

I AM ME is a declaration of self-esteem, stating in part, that "In all the world there is no one else exactly like me and everything that comes out of me is authentically mine because I alone chose it…" 23 x 35 inches, full color, $3.95 or 17 x 23 inches, $3.50

THE FIVE FREEDOMS offers the freedom to see and hear, say, feel, ask, and take risks for a better you. 23 x 35 inches, full color, $3.95

PEOPLE is gorgeously illustrated with a scene of natural beauty and includes Virginia's words "People need to see themselves as miracles and worthy of love." 23 x 35 inches, full color, $3.95

MAKING CONTACT illustrates what Virginia believes is the greatest gift one can give or receive. 23 x 35 inches, full color, $3.95

GOALS offers an answer to the question of how to make loving, appreciating, joining, inviting, leaving, and criticizing one another a truly enriching experience. 23 x 35 inches, full color, $3.95

WORLD PEACE is Virginia's pledge for peace, and includes the wise words "World peace begins at home." 23 x 35 inches, full color, $3.95

CELESTIAL ARTS
P.O. Box 7123, Berkeley, CA 94707   Phone Orders: (800) 841-BOOK